Also by Les Murray

Conscious and Verbal

Conscious and Verbal

Les Murray

Farrar, Straus and Giroux / *New York*

Farrar, Straus and Giroux
19 Union Square West, New York 10003

M964c

Distributed in Canada by Douglas & McIntyre Ltd.
Printed in the United States of America
Originally published in 2000 by Duffy & Snellgrove, Australia
Published in the United States by Farrar, Straus and Giroux
First American edition, 2001

ACKNOWLEDGEMENTS

Poems in this collection have previously appeared in *The Adelaide Review*, *The Age*, *Armidale Independent*, *The Australian*, *A Paean for Peter Porter*, ed. Anthony Thwaite (Bridgewater Press), *The Canberra Times*, *Caveat Lector*, *Cordite*, *Double Take*, *Epic Poise: in memoriam Ted Hughes*, *Forward Anthology: Best Poems of 1995*, *Grand Street*, *Granta*, *Great Lakes Advocate*, *Good Weekend*, *Harper's Magazine*, *Heat*, *Hesh*, *Kunapipi*, *Los Angeles Times*, *Masthead*, *New Exeter Book of Riddles*, ed. Lawrence Sail, *The New Yorker*, *Novocastrian Tales*, *The Paris Review*, *Planet*, *PN Review*, *Poetry Review*, *Poetry London Review*, *Poetry Scotland*, *Printed Matter* (Japan), *Quadrant*, *The Reader*, *Rialto*, *Salt*, *Scintilla*, *Stand*, *Sunday Times*, *Sunraysia Daily*, *Sydney Morning Herald*, *The Times Literary Supplement*, *Upstart*, *Verandah*, *The West Australian* and *The West Highland Free Press*, and many have been broadcast by the ABC and BBC.

Library of Congress Cataloging-in-Publication Data
Murray, Les A., 1938–
    Conscious and verbal / Les Murray.— 1st American ed.
      p. cm.
    ISBN 0-374-12882-0 (hardcover : alk. paper)
    I. Title.

PR9619.3.M83 C66 2001
821'.914—dc21

                          2001040222

Designed by Jonathan D. Lippincott

To the glory of God

Contents

Conscious and Verbal

Amanda's Painting

In the painting, I'm seated in a shield,
coming home in it up a shadowy river.
It is a small metal boat lined in eggshell
and my hands grip the gunwale rims. I'm
a composite bow, tensioning the whole boat,
steering it with my gaze. No oars, no engine,
no sails. I'm propelling the little craft with speech.
The faded rings around my loose bulk shirt
are of five lines each, a musical lineation,
and the shirt is apple-red, soaking in salt birth-sheen
more liquid than the river. My cap is a teal mask
pushed back so far that I can pretend it is headgear.
In the middle of the river are cobweb cassowary trees
of the South Pacific, and on the far shore rise
dark hills of the temperate zone. To these, at this
moment in the painting's growth, my course is slant
but my eye is on them. To relax, to speak European.

One Kneeling, One Looking Down

Half-buried timbers chained corduroy
lead out into the sand
which bare feet wincing Crutch and Crotch
spurn for the summer surf's embroidery
and insects stay up on the land.

A storm engrossing half the sky
in broccoli and seething drab
and standing on one foot over the country
burrs like a lit torch. Lightning
turns air to elixir at every grab

but the ocean sky is untroubled blue
everywhere. Its storm rolls below:
sand clouds raining on sacred country
drowned a hundred lifetimes under sea.
In the ruins of a hill, channels flow,

and people, like a scant palisade
driven in the surf, jump or sway
or drag its white netting to the tide line
where a big man lies with his limbs splayed,
fingers and toes and a forehead-shine

as if he'd fallen off the flag.
Only two women seem aware of him.
One says *But this frees us. I'd be a fool —*
Say it with me, says the other. *For him to revive*
we must both say it. Say Be alive. —

> *But it was our own friends who got*
> *him with a brave shot, a clever shot. —*
> *Those are our equals: we scorn them*
> *for being no more than ourselves.*
> *Say it with me. Say Be alive. —*

Elder sister, it is impossible. —
Life was once impossible. And flight. And speech.
It was impossible to visit the moon.
The impossible's our summoning dimension.
Say it with me. Say Be alive again. —

The younger wavers. She won't leave
nor stop being furious. The sea's vast
catchment of light sends ashore a roughcast
that melts off every swimmer who can stand.
Glaring through slits, the storm moves inland.

The younger sister, wavering, shouts *Stay dead!*
She knows how impossibility
is the only door that opens.
She pities his fall, leg under one knee,
but her power is his death, and can't be dignified.

Bottles in the Bombed City

Manchester, 1996

They gave the city a stroke. Its memories
are cordoned off. They could collapse on you.

Water leaks into bricks of the workers' century
and every meaning is blurred. No word in Roget

now squares with another. If the word is Manchester
it may be Australia, where that means sheets and towels.

To give the city a stroke, they mixed a lorryload
of henbane and meadowsweet oil and countrified her.

Now Engels supports only Max: and the British Union
of beautiful ceramics is being shovelled up,

blue-green tiles of the Corn Exchange,
umber gloss bricks of the Royal Midland Hotel.

Unmelting ice everywhere, and loosened molecules.
When the stroke came, every bottle winked at its neighbour.

The Margin of Difference

One and one make two,
the literalist said.
So far they've made five billion,
said the lateralist, or ten
times that, if you count the dead.

A Reticence

After a silver summer
of downpour, cement-powder autumn
set in its bag. Lawns turned crunchy
but the time tap kept dribbling away.

The paddocks were void as that evening
in early childhood when the sun
was rising in the west,
round and brimming as the factory furnace door,

as I woke up after sickness.
Then it was explained to me
that I'd slept through from morning
and I sobbed because I'd missed that day,

my entire lovely day.
Without you, it might have been a prophecy.

Travels with John Hunter

We who travel between worlds
lose our muscle and bone.
I was wheeling a barrow of earth
when agony bayoneted me.

I could not sit, or lie down,
or stand, in Casualty.
Stomach-calming clay caked my lips,
I turned yellow as the moon

and slid inside a CAT-scan wheel
in a hospital where I met no one
so much was my liver now my dire
preoccupation. I was sped down a road

of treetops and fishing-rod lightpoles
toward the three persons of God
and the three persons of John Hunter
Hospital. Who said We might lose this one.

Twenty days or to the heat-death
of the Universe have the same duration:
vaguely half an hour. I awoke
giggling over a joke

about Paul Kruger in Johannesburg
and missed the white court stockings
I half remembered from my prone
still voyage beyond flesh and bone.

I asked my friend who got new lungs
How long were you crazy, coming back?
Five days, he said. Violent and mad.
Fictive Afrikaner police were at him,

not unworldly Oom Paul Kruger.
Valerie, who had sat the twenty days
beside me, now gently told me tales
of my time-warp. The operative canyon

stretched, stapled, with dry roseate walls
down my belly. Seaweed gel
plugged views of my pluck and offal.
Some accident had released flora

who live in us and will eat us
when we stop feeding them the earth.
I'd rehearsed to private office of the grave,
ceased excreting, made corpse gases

all while liana'd in tubes
and overseen by cockpit instruments
that beeped or struck up Beethoven's
Fifth at behests of fluid.

I also hear when I lay lipless
and far away I was anointed
first by a mild metaphoric church
then by the Church of no metaphors.

Now I said, signing a Dutch contract
in a hand I couldn't recognise,
let's go and eat Chinese soup
and drive to Lake Macquarie. Was I

not renewed as we are in Heaven?
In fact I could hardly endure
Earth gravity, and stayed weak and cranky
till the soup came, squid and vegetables,

pure Yang. And was sane thereafter.
It seemed I'd also travelled
in a Spring-in-Winter love-barque of cards,
of flowers and phone calls and letters,

concern I'd never dreamed was there
when black kelp boiled in my head.
I'd awoken amid my State funeral,
nevermore to eat my liver

or feed it to the Black Dog, depression
which the three Johns Hunter seem
to have killed with their scalpels:
it hasn't found its way home,

where I now dodder and mend
in thanks for devotion, for the ambulance
this time, for the hospital forklift,
for pethidine, and this face of deity:

not the foreknowledge of death
but the project of seeing conscious life
rescued from death defines and will
atone for the human.

Drought Dust on the Crockery

Things were not better
when I was young:
things were poorer and harsher,
drought dust on the crockery,
and I was young.

The Harleys

Blats booted to blatant
dubbin the avenue dire
with rubbings of Sveinn Forkbeard
leading a black squall of Harleys
with Moe Snow-Whitebeard and

Possum Brushbeard and their ladies
and, sphincter-lipped, gunning,
massed leather muscle on a run,
on a roll, Santas from Hell
like a whole shoal leaning

wide-wristed, their tautness stable
in fluency, fast streetscape dwindling,
all riding astride, on the outside
of sleek grunt vehicles, woman-clung,
forty years on from Marlon.

Aurora Prone

The lemon sunlight poured out far between things
inhabits a coolness. Mosquitoes have subsided,
flies are for later heat.
Every tree's an auburn giant with a dazzled face
and the back of its head to an infinite dusk road.
Twilights broaden away from our feet too
as rabbits bounce home up defiles in the grass.
Everything widens with distance, in this perspective.
The dog's paws, trotting, rotate his end of infinity
and dam water feels a shiver few willow drapes share.
Bright leaks through their wigwam re-purple the skinny beans
then rapidly the light tops treetops and is shortened
into a day. Everywhere stands pat beside its shadow
for the great bald radiance never seen in dreams.

Best Western

The calm couple have no objection
and the baby, he looks keen
to see a smoker hunch in from the snow
and fatten a patchwork quilt in the straw
of their kerbside Nativity scene.

The Instrument

Who reads poetry? Not our intellectuals;
they want to control it. Not lovers, not the combative,
not examinees. They too skim it for bouquets
and magic trump cards. Not poor schoolkids
furtively farting as they get immunized against it.

Poetry is read by the lovers of poetry
and heard by some more they coax to the café
or the district library for a bifocal reading.
Lovers of poetry may total a million people
on the whole planet. Fewer than the players of *skat*.

What gives them delight is a never-murderous skim
distilled, to verse mainly, and suspended in rapt
calm on the surface of paper. The rest of poetry
to which this was once integral still rules
the continents, as it always did. But on condition now

that its true name's never spoken: constructs, feral poetry,
the opposite but also the secret of the rational.
And who reads these? Ah, the lovers, the schoolkids,
debaters, generals, crime-lords, everybody reads them:
Porsche, lift-off, Gaia, Cool, patriarchy.

Among the feral stanzas are many that demand your flesh
to embody themselves. Only completed art
free of obedience to its time can pirouette you
through and athwart the larger poems you are in.
Being outside all poetry is an unreachable void.

Why write poetry? For the weird unemployment.
For the painless headaches, that must be tapped to strike
down along your writing arm at the accumulated moment.
For the adjustments after, aligning facets in a verb
before the trance leaves you. For working always beyond

your own intelligence. For not needing to rise
and betray the poor to do it. For a non-devouring fame.
Little in politics resembles it: perhaps
the Australian colonists' re-inventing of the snide
far-adopted secret ballot, in which deflation could hide

and, as a welfare bringer, shame the mass-grave Revolutions,
so axe-edged, so lictor-y.
Was that moral cowardice's one shining world victory?
Breathing in dream-rhythm when awake and far from bed
evinces the gift. Being tragic with a book on your head.

Our Week in Grand Luxe

After Waterloo, the Channel
Tunnel was eventless experience:
we sloped down out of a Picardy
called Kent, talked beside blur
and emerged in a Kent called Picardy
but then the train began
to outrun nearby cars and
stop aeroplanes in the sky.
It began flying on earth
towards the portals of Paris
and everything, hamlets, trees, fields,
was left in an arrowy fallback
that only the suburbs could restrain.
Then we tumbled in a *valse*
à mille temps across the city,
paid off the taxi and rolled out
on a wingless plane for Avignon
over prairies and bisected hills
and sat up for hours where nothing
could join us from outside
without killing us, till we were in
the Province where pale rock has windows
and mortise-holes for coffins in it
and bubble-powdered speedy water
is guttered to carry cool through towns
built in a language they've stopped speaking.

There was knocking of steel boules
in shade until, in gloved unison,
domes of polished metal were raised
on Sèvres of festivity, on picnics
with galantines and counter-tenor,
on buses up a teetering road
to the high mountaintop where Petrarch,
first to climb a mountain just to write of it,

glimpsed the vision of tourism
and down to an evening-green
roof of fruiting cherry branches,
dense-spattered in human grazing reach
before more ortolans, more cabernets.
There was never snobbery, from our expert
carers. Friendly and artisanal,
their menus carried credits like films.
And when it was all achieved,
laudations, responses, evening brain-fog
from speaking literary languages,
we saw the Pope's emptied donjon and
St Bénézet's bridge, that stops short.

Spital Tower

i.m. Sorley MacLean, 1911–96

A cloister below
the Cheviot Hills
once sheltered lepers
but the Church dissolved
and the lepers died.
All over Northern Europe
the helpless died.

The cloister reared up
on end, against raiders,
then sank to a farmstead.
Murrays were in it
but poverty blew us
out of peasanthood
toward the Antipodes.

To no part of Europe
is our country antipodal:
its counter-foot
is the mid-Atlantic.

Where the great Gaelic poet
has gone, that's Antipodes,
Antipodes to everywhere.
Horror to the fortunate,
to the helpless, harbour:
death makes us all emigrants.

I pray where he is
excels modern doctrine
as his lines left on earth
out-glory his Spain.
I mourn, MacGillEain,
that my sleep under scalpels
meant I missed reading with you.

Now turning your pages
will be as if I riffled
the Northern Lights
and heard their language.

Rodd Island Wedding

On your wedding day, women were seated
on the Harbour, resting their oars.
Single sculls, in the grace of that spelling,
their canoes, slim as compass needles,
pointed at sandstone black with water,
at balconies and wharves and houses,
at sunny bays and lawn-set madhouses,
those châteaux of the upper Harbour,
at the tensioned bridges and their opposites.

Aqaba! A snorkel cleared its throat
and there you were, facing castanets of focus
on your wedding island. Since you'd become happy,
you told me, you'd stopped writing poems.
I should wish you a long silence. I do,
I do, if you mean it. The ribbed iron
feast-hall cruised through courses and clapping
like an airship under fans. The sportswomen
bent, and reached for distance like thistledowns.

Music to Me Is Like Days

Once played to attentive faces
music has broken its frame
its bodice of always-weak laces
the entirely promiscuous art
pours out in public spaces
accompanying everything, the selections
of sex and war, the rejections.
To jeans-wearers in zipped sporrans
it transmits an ideal body
continuously as theirs age. Warrens
of plastic tiles and mesh throats
dispense this aural money
this sleek accountancy of notes
deep feeling adrift from its feelers
thought that means everything at once
like a shrugging of cream shoulders
like paintings hung on park mesh
sonore doom soneer illy chesh!
they lost the off switch in my lifetime
the world reverberates with Muzak
and Prozac. As it doesn't with poe-zac
(I did meet a Miss Universe named Verstak).
Music to me is like days
I rarely catch who composed them
if one's sublime I think God
my life-signs suspend. I nod
it's like both Stilton and cure
from one harpsichord-hum:
penicillium—
then I miss the Köchel number.
I scarcely know whose performance
of a limpid autumn noon is superior
I gather timbre outranks rhumba.
I often can't tell days apart
they are the consumers, not me

in my head collectables decay
I've half-heard every piece of music
the glorious big one with voice
the gleaming instrumental one, so choice
the hypnotic one like weed-smoke at a party
and the muscular one out of farty
cars that goes Whudda Whudda
Whudda like the compound oil heart
of a warrior not of this planet.

Coolongolook Timber Mill

Down a road padlocked now
steel disks and weeds sprawled
in a room whose rusty hair
was iron cornrows, and its brow

a naily timber lintel
under which I'd gaze across
the river at Midge Island
as the tide turned on its pintle

and atoms would be dancing
like mayflies in the dusk
at the exact same speed as
gold roubles once spread glancing

around inch-freeboard puntloads
of sleepers axe trimmed
for Wittgenstein and Company
building the Siberian railroads

and black saws' sharkmouth edges
kept pipe-stuffers careful
up skids from sawdust-sized
shimmering of midges

then living drills were screwed
from punk wood to eat
by men wearing genitals; their
fish spears twitched like sedges

and the ocean sprawled in sight
gull-squealing, then weeks away
and the night sky quivered
with the vanished river's fleet

—a city man bought
the mill land for ten times
its price, and let the mill
fall down. But I have kept it.

Incunabular

Tom Fisher was my Grail King:
he endowed the Gothic library
to which my life had been pointing.
His high sandstone box held the Culture
bush folk were scorned for lacking.

On its milk-glass stack levels I still
hear stiletto heels clacking,
glass floors for the light to perfuse,
not for voyeurs: you could only
make out the sex of shoes.

The lipsticked gargoyle downstairs
kissed much social ascent.
Above, I'd browse beside the point
power made, for the points it didn't.
Reflex, more than intent.

The reading-room beam supported heraldry
and a roof like a steep tent.
Mine was a plan-free mass querying
of condensed humans off the shelves,
all numbered, the tribal, the elderly.

Knowledge was the gait of compressed selves
and poetry seemed windows of italic
inset in grievous prose
which served it and mastered it:
few grapes for many rows.

Students murmured airily of the phallic
they were going to be marked by
but the shelvers book-trolleys were parked by
closed gaping tomes and stood them drily back,
vogue, value, theory.

The stacks clanged down metal stairs
to floors below reality,
to books in dragon-buckram, books like dreams,
antiphonaries and grimoires,
philologies with pages still uncut:

my blade made a sound like *rut*.
I never used the catalogue,
it held no serendipities.
The lateral book's the tip: it is
the seminal one near the one set.

You must range real shelves to find it.
Strict exams could have excluded me;
soon they did weed out my sort.
Critique closed over poetry,
the hip proved very straight.

What our donjon of kisses and cribs held
they say now will go on line.
This does not light my taper.
Others may have my joys at home? Fine.
But I surfed the true paper.

A Deployment of Fashion

In Australia, a lone woman
is being crucified by the Press
at any given moment.

With no unedited right
of reply, she is cast out
into Aboriginal space.

It's always for a defect in weeping:
she hasn't wept on cue
or she won't weep correctly.

There's a moment when the sharks are
still butting her, testing her protection,
when the Labor Party, or influence,

can still save her. Not the Church,
not other parties. Even at that stage
few men can rescue her.

Then she goes down, overwhelmed
in the feasting grins of pressmen,
and Press women who've moved

from being owned by men
to being owned by fashion,
these are more deeply merciless.

She is rogue property,
she must be taught her weeping.
It is done for the millions.

Sometimes the millions join in
with jokes: how to get a baby
in the Northern Territory? Just stick

your finger down a dingo's throat.
Most times, though, the millions
stay money, and the jokes

are snobbish media jokes:
Chemidenko. The Oxleymoron.
Spittle, like the flies on Black Mary.

After the feeding frenzy
sometimes a ruefully balanced last lick
precedes the next selection.

Prime Numbers

What are you doing now, Les?

Normally I live in the country,
work, garden, parry thrusts from the *Herald*,
but two days a week I fly in
to a cubicle in the Stacked City,
an every-coloured brick university
that is built on top of itself
like a brain's lobes and evolutionary layers
on the last rock before Botany Bay.

The inner streets of this oppidum
are paved with grey carpet, and inmates
lie on them for cool negotiations
or to write in big pads. Footsteps with vocal
animate the stairs and little squares;
odd walls not yet built over
catch sun and frecklings of leaves;
a coffee shop may form round a stairwell.

My cubicle briefly bears my name
but no dates yet. Today I compose
in there about a former madhouse,
still meshed and brass-keyed when I met
all three of a shattered great poet.
He died before they let the mad out
to home like themes in family novels,
to swap locked for liberated hells.

Now the place is ochre, after cream,
and writers read there, beneath airliners
that brew up from under the horizon
and score prodigious hyphens through poems.
My dapper friend Philip appeared there,
nine years up-ramp in his wheelchair

from a stroke, to a dry chin, to language,
to his first new poem, just written.

The same week, a boy-man who didn't
speak for years told me *Cars in the mirror*
drive on the right, the noon sun's south:
mirrors are like the northern hemisphere.
A million self-rescues so vertical
don't multiply. Each one is the shining one.
Love poured out on them also doesn't
subtract from the numbers they've attained.

Back above the racehorse-named streets
in Overlap City, I'm really a specimen,
a mountain to geographers. But Louise's friend
Sarah yarned with me, Annette too (God and Mary to her!)
and poet Hazel, and Peter the biographer—
all these the day after the burial
of Mother Theresa, whose real grace
lay in knowing how little to generalise.

To Me You'll Always Be Spat

Baby oyster, little grip,
settling into your pinch of shape
on a flooded timber rack:

little living gravel
I'm the human you need,
one who won't eat you,

not with much relish, even
when you're maturely underexercised
inside your knuckle sandwich.

Bloodless sheep's eye, never
appear in a bottle. Always bring
ice, lemon and your wonky tub.

You have other, non-food powers:
your estuaries are kept clean as crystal,
you eat through your jacuzzi,

you make even the non-sexy
think of a reliable wet
machine of pleasure,

truly inattentive students
of French hope they heard right,
that you chant in the arbours.

Commandant-of-convicts Wallis
who got the Wallis name unfairly
hated, had you burnt alive

in millions to make mortar.
May you now dance in the streets
and support a gross of towns!

The Disorderly

We asked How old will you be
in the year Two Thousand?
Sixty-two. Sixty. Fifty-nine.

Unimaginable. We started running
to shin over the sliprails
of a wire fence. You're last!—

It's all right: I'll be first in Heaven!
and we jogged on to school
past a yellow-flowering guinea vine.

Cattle stood propped on the mountain.
We caught a day-blind glider possum
and took him to school. Only later

at the shoe-wearing edge of our world
did we meet kids who thought everything
ridiculous. They found us incredible.

Cream-handed men in their towns
never screamed Christ-to-Jesus! at the hills
with diabetes breath, nor talked fight

or Scotch poetry in scared timber rooms.
Such fighters had lost, we realised,
but we had them to love

or else we'd be mongrels.
This saved our souls later on,
sometimes, crossing the cousinless

detective levels of the world
to the fat-free denim culture,
that country of the Attitudes.

Five Postcards

Having run herself up out of
plush, the white-cheeked wallaby
sits between her haunches
like an old-country tailor behind
her outstretched last yard, her tail,
and hems it with black fingers.

_____

Cosmic apples by Cézanne:
their colours, streaming, hit
wavelengths of crimson and green
in the yellowy particle-wind.
Slant, parallel and pouring,
every object's a choke-point of speeds.

_____

The kitchens of this 18th century
Oxford college are ten metres high
by the squinch-eyed cooks basting
tan birds spiked in hundreds all over
the iron griddle before hellfire.
Below high lozengy church windows
others flour, fill, pluck. And this too
was the present once, that absolute of fools.

_____

1828. Timber slums of the future
top a ship of the line, which receives
more who might have stormed St James's.
Cheery washing lines signal they're bound
for the world's end, to seize there
the lands of unclothed aristos
rich in myth and formal grammar.

_____

A mirrory tar-top road across
a wide plain. Drizzling sky.
A bike is parked at a large book
turned down tent-fashion on the verge.
One emerging says *I read such crazy*
things in this book. "*Every bird*
has stone false teeth and enters
the world in its coffin." *That's in there.*

The Internationale

Baron Samedi, leaving the House of Lords,
shrugs on his shoulders and agrees to come.
Have you observed, he asks, *dat a tarantula
is built like, but nimbler than, a Rugby scrum?*

The Manche blows east like a billion tabloid pages,
annoying the Baron: *Sheer prose, dese Narrow Seas!*
but a cohort of Lundys leaps out of Leemavaddy
on an intricate tuning of spring steel in their knees.

Mardi, now svelte, hoists up a horizontal ballad
and ascends its couplets because the fire's at the top
but Macready with a wheedle of a reedy pitch-pipe conjures
the cobra whose head will fit his wet eye-socket. Pop!

Jeu d'Esprit and Jeu de Paume grace our company
and the Countess von Dredy informs us with some pain
that in Gold-Orange-Land is now the sour gherkin season.
She'd rather complete a Seminar than a Semaine.

Yall need some time on the low horse! Mardi cries
as they all skip around us with Sha-na-na and Boom!
Our energy shorten your lease of joy, cries the Baron.
But having summoned we, do you wish we trudge in gloom?

More than an Obiter Dichter

for Peter Porter

Peter, you're in the dictionary!
It doesn't say what you mean
but you're noted for urbane wit in
the Macquarie, second edition.

Another friend's daughter found my
name in there, and the year I died
already past. With that behind me,
hey, I'm invincible, I cried.

It's right, as you know: our true
poetry follows our deaths,
It's fun to write the rest alive, though,
bibbling among the shibboleths,

weaving between our epitaphs.
Like a fast waterbird leading the dawn
in a string of musket-flashes across Garda
what we have written we have drawn.

May you reach your own century from this one.
Thank you for much hospitality.
A pillar of good talk all night
you were, and of company by day.

Master poet, Peter, you're this rock
tickled by roses in their climb;
you're our blue-edged flag, our fore-runner
first off the adzed blocks of home.

Be Italy and music for all readers:
Australia's no place to be Australian.
Let's tussle in a jar again sometime.
Thank you for my start in London.

The Water Plough

That was the Iron Age all right.
I'm glad it's in the museum.
Like that iron dam-sinking scoop
the weight of an Indian Chief motorbike
in there, from back before dozers.
I trained on that, cleaning dams.

Every five or ten years
you had to scoop out the silt
and stinking slop from a dam
or you'd have a paddy, not a pond.
First thing, you'd break through the wall
and let the water go like a culvert
you hoped you could seal up again.

The horse you yoked for the scooping
had to be a goer, but smart
enough to stop short at a word.
The trace-chains came off a swingle-tree
way ahead at his heels, and the timber
steering-shafts stretched you like flying,
your hands were so far apart.

You'd skim round the edges first,
shaving off the lashes of reeds
and dumping them with a twist over
and a twist back to keep the chains
uncrossed. And then you'd face
the dam bottom, the eel jelly.

What you did in there wasn't walk
nor swim, it was trail belly-down
with stabs for purchase with your boots
and curses and sprawls and swerving
as your big two-handed cruet

filled and piled and overflowed
and you'd lie down on the shafts
to keep its front edge up and clear
and swim it out to the paddock
to spill there, and the eels kicking
like nerves in it, biting at the dogs.

And that was when it went right.
However it went, you'd come up
out of the lost bedsteads and bones
with a suit of slime all over you
the colour of a Box Brownie photo
and thick as beef, smelling aluminium,
or yellow pug with leeches hooked like bait to you.
You'd glop around, weighing tons.
No hose, no showers then. A mate
or your wife might bucket your face
clear for tea and a smoke
as you caked and stiffened, then back:
Into it, son: you wasn't born dry!

Making the dams in the first place,
that was the bastard of a job.
You'd be stagger-walking, on dry land
at least, but the scoop might
stop curling the dirt and nosedive
for Hell any minute, and stick
and break the harness or your shoulders.
A quick enough kick-up of the shafts
could toss you over them like over
the horns of a bullock at the Show
and it was iron, that ridge ground.

The edge of a dragline scoop got
so sharpened, grinding gravel and stone,
it could have cut a man in two
easily if he got in front of it.
No wonder it glided purring through
spewy stuff, and snoring through
the better loam and clay, and left them

all polished like tiles, on a good day.
Butchered like shellholes on a bad day
groaning and screaming like them, too.

From the off you had to keep separate
the loam and leaf-mould so they didn't
get into the clay wall that you keyed,
levelled with just your eye, which is water
after all, and walked the horse over
and over, and hand-rammed, and hoped would hold,
and half the time it didn't hold.

You got the blind staggers from tiredness
but I admit I liked the work, odd times,
spreading the hard knuckles of ridges
to fit a dam between, or giving
full play to a soak. Building with the country,
not on it. Building and reshaping it,
cuttings and bywashes and ramps,
finding the walls it would agree to,
stopping the chainsaws of erosion-water,
arresting them to spoons of sky light
for cattle and dingoes and birds
and turtles and blue lilies with leaves
like the tin stump-caps of houses.

Now the green bulldozer dams everywhere
are lakes to the puddleholes we made.
Fly over the country with the sun low
and it's all like gripped with fingernails:
gleams hang up on every allotment
to be some family's park pond
but it's still our idea
of making flood rain stay and perform
before it got off the continent
or deep into it, to the great still swirls.

The Great Hall of Chlorine

It is the great hall of Chlorine,
the Aquatic Centre. Light shaking all over the walls,
people of bleach and biscuit pad on raw feet
and children splat diamante. Many intently surge
out of deep trampolines of wavering.
Women adjust harness, some karate-chop at speed;
men exude their inner showers on the sauna's wooden shelves.
Heads are calm in the laundry-boiling of the spa
and a rare drip falls bling!
from the loose leaves of the ceiling.

A nonwhite family comes in, and glances vaguely,
aware some may still notice. The mother
picks at her plastic wrist-tie, her entry ticket.
Hardly anyone looks; no children do,
but through being of an age, or an education,
a few are subtly forced to notice. Many
of the white people, so called, are darker, from the sun,
but this is Race. This carries accusation.
Intellectuals invented race, and for centuries supplied
the terrible theory which deflected chains and conquest
away from the Modern, onto Primitives.
Now they turn the same weapon on their poor relations.
Anything these brown folk say, any hurt in their eyes
may be used against us.

Imagery has stopped. We're furtive in our minds.
What reaches of Gondwanaland are ancestral to these
I don't know. Whatever Race is, I read it poorly.
If their forebears once stood behind trees on their shore
watching nightmare develop like a Polaroid from seaward, what
stopped them charging, burning its stores, clubbing, killing
in that last window moment? That it was also riveting?
Occasionally some were decisively conservative
but it always came to that same moment again:

you had been after game, or making men, and the
excreting spirits were back, with their offering hands.

When the Martians come, they're like a university.
Their genes wink to instinct, their flashes shiver the gods.
Every mind intuits its escape from a perfect world.
But it goes on. The Martians are setting exams
in their own language. The Fail mark is terrible: epidemic,
the swerving muskets, death in a bag of flour.
The ancient poetry totters—but new laughs get learned,
jobs tried, worlds pictured, and brave ambitious women
come to borrow seed at the edge of spaceship tents,
things better known on the low horse than the high horse.

Few horses come into the great hall of the Chlorine:
better not to bring them.
Nothing in the water feeds Race. A little of the sun
pouring in through wiped walls may be kin to it,
but that family the Race dog followed in has merged
in the swimming noise of this mall, handling blue and yellow
floats that mark the lapping lanes. They plunge under ropes
and separate into their ages, over by the wheelchair hoist.
If I met them, we might become good friends
if we could cross that land, proxy-farmed for indignation,
that lies between us.

A Dog's Elegy

The civil white-pawed dog who'd strain
to make speech-like sounds to his humans
lies buried in the soil of a slope
that he'd tear down on his barking runs.

He hated thunder and gunshot
and would charge off to restrain them.
A city dog too alive for backyards,
we took him from the pound's Green Dream

but now his human name melts off him;
he'll rise to chase fruit bats and bees;
the coral tree and the African tulip
will take him up, and the prickly tea trees.

Our longhaired cat who mistook him
for an Alsatian flew up there full tilt
and teetered in top twigs for eight days
as a cloud, distilling water with its pelt.

The cattle suspect the Dog lives
but three kangaroos stood in our pasture
this daybreak, for the first time in memory,
eared gazing wigwams of fur.

László

One crepe-myrtle tree's already mirrored
in the grass by bloom it has shed,
tissue flowerets the exact mauve of gloves
that adjust the coffined dead.

Now it's evening. Cuisine on television:
artful pinches in Republic-flag liquid
on vast plates. I thought I would find
thistles in Scotland, too, but I never did.

Last night I met Lesley Murray.
She was my junior. Logically so.
Male Leslies crashed with Leslie Howard
in '43. And he was a László.

My friend's mother, seeing a woman shot,
split, and knew detachment from then on.
I marvelled She remembers when hers started!—
I watch myself writing this down.

Big Shame

When Dad and I first drove to Sydney
we shared billy tea by the kerb
brewed with water a housewife boiled for us.
Too flash for him, a café in a suburb,

though he could charm them dewy when he tried.
Same with all Up Home advice, where to eat
or stay, in the Big Smoke: it's always
cheap holes where slurs die of defeat.

One dictionary awards rural-poor speech
entire to the Black folk who share it:
box up, walk off, bad friends, Poor, growl,
cheeky, hollow, in with, hunt, quiet—

Define me all those, or spare the Proletariat.
It's called Big Shame, my poison-brother fellow
says, this feeling abashed by proper people.
Before Racist and Beaut Authentic, we were Low

for which you get sentenced to the past
—you never see the court—
to smokes, to single beds in plywood rooms,
to union legends, to sashcord round your port.

poison-brother: brother-in-law; an Aboriginal term arising from kinship rules under which
in-laws are avoided.

The Sunraysia Poems

Asparagus Bones

Thirstland talc light
haunted the bush horizons
all day. As it softened
into blusher we drove out
through gardens that are farms
past steeped sultana frames
to a red-earth dune
flicked all over with water
to keep it tightly knitted
in orange and avocado trees
black-green and silver green
above trickling dust. My friend
fetched a box of fossil bones
from the unlocked half-million
of the coolroom there: asparagus
for his banquet kitchen,
no-one around, no dog,
then we drove where biceps
of river water swelled
through a culvert, and bulges
of turbulence hunted swirls
just under their moon skin,
and we mentioned again
unsecured farm doors, open
verandahs, separate houses,
emblems of a good society.

Oasis City, Mildura, Victoria

Rose-red city in the angles of a cut-up
green anthology: grape stanzas, citrus strophes,
I like your dirt cliffs and chimney-broom palm trees,

your pipe dream under dust, in its heads of pressure.
I enjoy your landscape blown from the Pleistocene
and roofed in stick forests of tarmacadam blue.

Your river waltzed round thousands of loops to you
and never guessed. Now it's locked in a Grand Canal,
aerated with paddlewheels, feeder of kicking sprays,

its willows placid as geese outspread over young
or banner-streamed under flood. Hey, rose-red city
of the tragic fountain, of the expensive brink,

of crescent clubs, of flags basil-white-and-tomato,
I love how you were invented and turned on:
the city as equipment, unpacking its intersections.

City dreamed wrongly true in Puglia and Antakya
with your unemployed orange-trunks globalised out of the ground,
I delight in the mountains your flat scrub calls to mind

and how you'd stack up if decanted over steep relief.
I praise your camel-train skies and tanglefoot red-gums
and how you mine water, speed it to chrome lace and slow it

to culture's ingredients. How you learn your tolerance
on hideous pans far out, by the crystals of land sweat.
Along high-speed vistas, action breaks out of you,

but sweeter are its arrivals back inside
dust-walls of evergreen, air watered with raisins and weddings,
the beer of day pickers, the crash wine of night pickers.

Closer Links with Sunraysia

Hoofed beasts are year-round fires
devouring as high as they can reach,
hopeless to put out. Pink smoke
lifts off their terra cotta

but all fences have been torn out
and flocks, herds and horses banished
from this apricot country. Here
they've finished with the pastoral.

Downstream of this sprinkled terrain
merged desert rivers stop-go to Ocean
but the real Australian river,
the one made of hard labour and launched

with a tilt of a Chinese pole-bucket,
that one sets out for the human mouth
down a thousand asphalt beds
in squeaky crates and marshalled vintages.

The Bulb of the Darling Lily

Sitting round in the Grand Hotel
at Festival time. Another year
that Philip Hodgins can't be here.
Naming the festival after him
almost confirms that. But like his fine
drypoint poems, it lets him be somewhere.

Sitting around in the Grand
with the stained glass in the gaming room
an upwelling pattern of vivid cards
and the T-shaped lolly-coloured logo
of the TAB everywhere, the Tabaret.
All Victoria's become one casino.

Sitting around the Grand Hotel
adding antipasto to the impasto
of my mortal likeness, writing postcards
instead of going on the guided
Lake Mungo tour. Too reverential,
too sacred. No grinners out there laugh.

So, sitting around in the Grand
yarning with Mario, with Donna and Stefano
and descending to the lower kitchen
to meet Leopardo Leopardi, who isn't
posing in languor on a thorn-tree limb
though he has the build, but making gnocchi.

Sitting around the Grand Hotel, yarning
about river cod as big as seals
and the de-snagged inland waters
being re-snagged to let them breed,
shovel-mouthed, with the beady gape
and rejecting clamp of a critic.

The Newly Tragic Dodo

It's French for sleeping,
It's English for dead,
the first extinction
the regretful regretted.

Trustful island bird, flightless,
too long on its pat:
survivors-of-the-fittest
used to point to all that,

but approving any die-out's
now a thing you don't do;
evolution is racist
if you think it right through.

When we were tough
the dodo was grotesque,
fat, silly, comical—
now it's proud and brisk.

As any being becomes fashionable
its weight loses weight,
like the sea-supported whale
or the Carolina parrot.

The Mowed Hollow

When yellow leaves the sky
they pipe it to the houses
to go on making red
and warm and floral and brown
but gradually people tire of it,
return it inside metal, and go
to be dark and breathe watercolours.

Some yellow hangs on outside
forlornly tethered to posts.
Cars chase their own supply.

When we went down the hollow
under the stormcloud nations
the light was generalised there
from vague glass places in the trees
and the colours were moist and zinc,
submerged and weathered and lichen
with black aisles and white poplar blues.

The only yellow at all
was tight curls of fresh butter
as served on stainless steel
in a postwar café: cassia flowers,
soft crystal with caraway-dipped tongues,
butter mountains of cassia flowers
on green, still dewed with water.

Towards 2000

As that monster the Twentieth Century
sheds its leathers and chains, it will cry

Automatic weapons! I shot at
millions and they died. I kept doing it,

but most not ruled by uniforms ate well
in the end. And cool replaced noble.

Nearly every black-and-white Historic figure
will look compromised by their haircut and cigar-

ette. And the dead will grow remoter
among words like *pillow-sham* and *boater.*

You'll admit, the old century will plead,
I developed ways to see and hear the dead.

Only briefly will TV restrain Hitler
and Napoleon from having an affair.

I changed my mind about the retarded:
I ended great for those not the full quid.

You breathers, in your rhythmic inner blush,
you dismiss me, now I'm a busted flush,

but I brought cures, mass adventures—no one's fooled.
A line called Last Century will be ruled

across all our lives, lightly at first,
even as unwiring bottles cough

their corks out, and posh aerosols burst
and glasses fill and ding, and people quaff.

You Find You Can Leave It All

Like a charging man, hit
and settling face down in the ringing,
his cause and panic obsolete,

you find you can leave it all:
your loved people, pain, achievement
dwindling upstream of this raft-fall,

back with the dishes that translated
beasts and croplands into the ongoing
self-portrait your genes had mandated.

Ribbed fluorescent glare-panels flow
over you down urgent corridors,
dismissing midday outside. Slow,

they'd resemble wet spade-widths in a pit;
you've left grief behind you, for others;
your funeral: who'll know you'd re-planned it?

God, at the end of prose,
somehow be our poem—
When forebrainy consciousness goes

wordless selves it'd barely met,
inertias of rhythm, the life habit
continue the battle for you.

If enough of those hold
you may wake up in this world,
ache-boned, tear-sponged, dripped into:

Do you know your name? "Yes" won't do.
It's Before again, with shadow. No tunnels.
You are a trunk of prickling cells.

It's the evening of some day. But it's also
afterlife from here on, by that consent
you found in you, to going where you went.

The Derelict Milky Way

for Taree City Millennium Committee

Those estuaries of the east coast
with burnish over their olives and tans
from a sun that reads its days from right
to left, the Arab and Hebrew way;

each river's a trumpet with a sand mute,
its valves are lift bridges at upstream towns;
receding outbreaks of violent hessian
map a long industry called The Highway

and little crosses turbaned in wreath
along its verges mark traffic death,
all because trumpets are no longer blown,
some reckon. Because there's no agreed tune.

This coast was a cheek the Millennium
kissed early, on both of its dawns
as the Black Armband tightened and loosened
round throats, on our moral proscenium.

Such stuff was all Town, though, way back
when milk-lorries stacked can on can
bringing us in to learn from Shakespeare's
fifteen acts against one fat man.

For pelicans over bottle-coloured lakes
time doesn't count to a climax
then re-start, from no egg, in mid-air.
Eels scuttering on creek crossings don't care,

but a dog's nose snuggled to your bum
is a form of walking hand in hand
and all through the bricked enormous Hospital
cousins jink in wheeled beds from room to room.

I wish us all more truthful cousinship
of more races, in the centuries to come—
that's my boost. Beached lovers caress
like singing to each other in Braille

and *Wrong wrong!* the cattle grids sing
on sphinx-knee hills to the high plateau
and guitar-shaped helicopters peer, strumming,
for a pot crop in forests' cloud-shadow

but the big legal crop here is wilderness,
closing, in its solitudes and myriads,
on a Milky Way still settled by Australians
now portrayed kindly only in ads.

Literary Editor

He sits rejecting poems,
saying too much no,
a black pen in his hand
to score their lack of lo!
but then a magic word stands up
off the page: *candelaborough*—

it throws him out of kilter.
I've been too fine a filter.
Now see: the name of my true home.
It calls me! My native rococo!
Snug in his stamped envelope,
folds grimed like those in verses,

he rejects himself, bites a wet lip
and steering with his paperclip
lifts off for their rendezvous:
You edit me! You are my due!
Above the cirrus he traverses
we hear his fading blip.

The Relative Gold

Most white people had no relations,
some had things to live up or live down;
in the days of Black Tommy McPherson
the country was more like the town.

Black Tom was a sport in New England
with his red Spanish boots and his sash
but among those who have no relations
respect is called credit. Bare cash

will get you supplies and survival
depending what stories are told—
so Black Tommy reached into New England
and drew out alluvial gold.

Places lightning had shattered in water
and still winked among pebbles were the source
of his drinking with duffers and teamsters;
all this drew the blue Police Force

who badgered him under suspicion
and questioned him where his claim lay
but the claims he half made and grinned off
truly tangled their snarling assay.

No trackers, no vertical riding
in gorges traced the washed vein of worth
with which he was buying up dignity.
Next thing, blacks'd be sharing the earth!

Tom's one of the Tableland's richest men,
smiled gold expert Henry Grob.
Who'd begrudge a McPherson up here? laughed Tommy,
treat me right; I could give you a job.

But someone who sought other favour
or had their own notions of class
sidled round in the Bald Nob barroom
and got their hand near Tommy's glass.

The spiked drink that sent Tommy reeling
across the dray road to fall down
gave him visions of two troopers gloating
You look a real black now, you clown!

Tom McPherson was never seen working;
he rode a high horse like a lord,
so the police who never worked either
had arranged, and now shared, a reward.

One put a bullet through a lung:
That's for the times you got off! —
This is for Yugilbar sports day!
Tom's wit drowned in his agonised cough.

As half of New England bewailed him,
diggers, carriers and Cobb and Co. men
with relations and none declared Bald Nob Hotel
black, in the new jargon of then.

It broke and killed licensee McCormick,
it half starved his children and wife.
The tribal spouse Tommy had fought for
had more backup in her widowed life.

I was thinking about New England,
of the Buggs, the Wards and the Wrights,
how they'd all conjured gold from that country
by their different methods and lights.

I was thinking this when my credit cards
came up empty, and I was eyed
with that narrowed no-human-kin look
that would discount anything I tried.

All the gold I'd spun out of country
was imagery, remotely extolled,
but Tommy McPherson sported his with an air,
a black cousin with literal gold.

The Ice Indigene

Prone on its wrists, beige Bear
chins the ice, its shoulders a roll bar.
Its grand wheel-arch hindquarters

are flexed to propel this fur car
at you in a gallop
           or bouncing in a lope
after oil seals who die for you.

Snow-mortared intelligent loner,
dope-eyed, with hair in his fur.
Abhor his sleeves upraised in preaching!

Arctos can drive on water
or canter the tilting platforms
amassed on the dome of ocean.

On the whitening blue-white, where landmarks
aren't made of land, and vanish,
she can live without help.

She wakes to motherhood. Gaffs
tip her gloves. Her diet is
all meat, with guts for vegetables.

She can wrest a red whale off Inuit,
appal their harpoons,
           leave them Nunuvut.

Berg-drifted to a grass shore, she'd
raven on Norsemen, those poetic terse men.
Caught flatfooted, the snowdrift garbageman

may totter cavern-voiced,
tall as tractor cabins
in the aurora's scope light,

then hibernate between divorcing
continents, in a helicopter sling.
He can be simple anywhere he's going.

The Day I Slept Like a Dolphin

The day I slept like a dolphin
I'd flown the Atlantic twice over
and come down in snow-rimmed Denver.
There I filled in both entry papers
and got called back: *Hey! You, Buddy!*
You didn't fill these out right!
It was true. Only the right hand
side of the Immigration form
and of the Customs form had writing.
I could explain that to you, I marvelled,
as he impatiently did not,
he of La Migra. *But I'd bore you*,
I added, and filled in the left questions.
Under an Atlantic of fatigue
one half of my brain had been sleeping
as the other kept watch and rose to breathe.
Next time, I'll peep, and get
a second, waking view of my dreams.

La Migra: Mexican slang for the U.S. Immigration Service.

The Rotterdam Flight Cage

Unexpected among Rotterdam's
steel-decked architectural cargo:
a flight cage three storeys high
built inside a theatre complex
and glazed on its snow-weather side.

It held a confetti of parrots
when I was there. Not burly
captains'-shoulder models, but small
taut pastel and nibble-mouthed Australians,
momentary foliage to polished stick boughs,

corellas, leeks, rosellas, budgerigars
which rose and jinked and showered
down again like crystalline themes
of badinage taken up and dropped
inside their day-and-night cylinder.

Well fed and I imagine all
European born, they were hardly
more imprisoned than most
little seed birds in the wild,
those whose aviary moves about

because it is the flock,
or ones whose whole life-territory
ranges from the verandah edge out
to the gloss-cardboard loquat tree,
or is two marsh fields a planet apart.

Safe from being frittered, in the powder
light of their deep tower they composed
in kinks, wing-leaves and creamy streaks
impressions of their inherent country,
like the stylised African moves

most humans now consciously do,
we being an African species.

Small Flag above the Slaughter

Perhaps a tribal kinship,
some indigenous skinship
is equivalent to the term our neighbour saw
fit to award his amiable then-fit successor,
now sick, whom he nurses:
He is my husband-in-law.

Downhill on Borrowed Skis

White mongrel I hate snow
wadded numbing mousse
grog face in a fur noose
the odd miraculous view
through glass or killing you
the only time I skied
I followed no skilled lead
but on parallel lent boards
fell straight down a hill
fell standing up by clenched will
very fast on toe-point swords
over logshapes and schist
outcrips crops it was no piste
nor had I had any drinks
wishing my ankles steel links
winging it hammer and Shazam
no stocks in afternoon mirk
every cloud-gap royally flash
like heading into a car crash
ayyy the pain! the paperwork!
my hands I didn't flail them
though neither left nor right
neither schuss nor slalom
my splitting splay twinned sled
pumping straining to spread
to a biplane wreck of snapped ligaments
all hell played with locked joints
but still I skidded down erect
in my long spill of grist
blinded hawk on a wrist
entirely unschooled unchecked
the worst going on not and not
happening no sprawl no bone-shot
till I stood on the flat
being unlatched and exclaimed at.

The Holy Show

I was a toddler, wet-combed
with my pants buttoned to my shirt
and there were pink and green lights, pretty
in the day, a Christmas-tree party
up the back of the village store.

I ran towards it, but big sad people
stepped out. They said over me *It's just, like,
for local kiddies* and *but let him join in*;
the kiddies looked frightened
and my parents, caught off guard

one beat behind me, grabbed me up
in the great shame of our poverty
that they talked about to upset themselves.
They were blushing and smiling, cursing me
in low voices *Little bugger bad boy!*

for thinking happy Christmas undivided,
whereas it's all owned, to buy in parcels
and have at home; for still not knowing
you don't make a holy show of your family;
outside it, there's only parry and front.

Once away, they angrily softened to
me squalling, because I was their kiddie
and had been right about the holy show
that models how the world should be
and could be, shared, glittering in near focus

right out to the Sex frontier.

The Good Plates

On the day of babyhood
the Christmas guest would come,
a soldier back from the war,
someone single, or far from home.

After new toys and ice cream,
midmorning those hot Decembers,
the family would turn ideal,
polite even to its members.

Still home, but genial, drought-free,
as the good plates came out;
angry topics winked as if forgiven
over cordials and Sheaf stout.

When all the Good Luck toasts failed
we in turn played guest
to old people in dark parlours
serving up their calm best,

then photos often show this person
among family, and loyal,
but chatting with some visible stranger
to mitigate the festival.

Passover night, Jews set a place
for Elijah the prophet.
If more than a twosome, perhaps,
no human circle is complete,

and one more's a way out of too many.
Come spirit, come witness:
family love's the point, or childhood,
but the guest is Christmas.

A Verb Agreement

After a windstorm, the first man
aloft in our broad silky-oak tree
was Andrew Lansdown the poet,
bearded and supple, nimbly
disinvolving wrecked branches
up where I couldn't clamber.

He asked for our chainsaw, but I
couldn't let him hazard an iamb or
a dactyl, nor far worse his
perched body of value and verses;
showering rubies were an image to terrify
even about an imagist so spry.

So, above my scattered choppings, he
hawked with a handsaw west-and-southerly
and went home to Susan with our thanks,
God-spared from caesuras or endstoppings.
The tree has twice since become
a Scala of ginger balconies, a palladium

as it does every October.
Birds with skin heads like the thumb
on a black hand interrogate its bloom
with dulcet commentary till it's sober
but, bat-nipped gold or greening out blue,
it glories like the kingdom within Andrew.

At the Swamping of Categories

With thanks and acknowledgements to Iris Chang

When the flag of the pool of blood
came up the Yangtze Valley
its soldiers were licensed to flow
into a great space of cruelty.
They filled canals with working men;

they transmitted their own DNA
then slaughtered the women who got it;
they widened the littlest girls
and halved them after with swords.
When the flag of the clot of blood

came up the Yangtze Valley
it flew above a tsunami
God waited for inertia or humans
to arrest, as with a wave of ocean.
When the red-dyed rice ball of the poor

fluttered below the walls of Nanjing
seven hundred thousand people
cowered, reassuring one another
as their own collapsed army changed clothes.
The Purple Mountain was burning

and the Emperor's troops entered the city
behind tracked one-eyed steel cars
that busted all bodies they reached
and the many more being made running.
This was old atomic war: humans as the atoms.

Of twenty-seven Westerners in the city
most were missionaries. Of YH God.
To head-severing contests, to mass shootings,
to screaming flagrante with impalements
these opposed a refusal of awe.

With nonbelievers and mild Christmas-keepers,
armed only with prestige and shouts
they patrolled the two-square-mile bounds
of the safety zone Wilson Mills devised.
They ran between machine guns and ranked men;

their eyes were the Vietnam TV
of thirty years later, to Christmas bayonets.
Pure bluff, scorned at first, the Safety Zone grew real:
some pronounced the reason *faith*, some *face*,
but John Rabe's swastika arm

day and night shielded a multitude.
Among Nazis, Oskar Schindler saved his thousand
and the Rabes their scores of thousands.
When the flag of the soldier's slapped face
sanctioned gut-pulling military dogs

Minnie Vautrin whose battery torch
was a light-sword to hack rapes apart,
James McCallum of the ambulance ploy,
Lewis Smythe, John Wilson the one surgeon,
these fought in the Iliad of peace,

Ernest Forster, John Magee who filmed it:
they were jostled, shot near, pitched down
HQ stairs, but their fiction held
the half of Nanjing that would survive
its slashed frosted-earth weeks of delirium.

Though all of Nanjing's twenty-seven
were prosperous, in ways snobbish, and white,
they kept alive three hundred thousand
people seen then as not their colour,
got them mouthfuls, and their plight to the world.

Trade, ideological war, and the A-bomb
have buried the International Committee
but, each against armed lewd thousands,
by such very odds,
they turned a glamorous rage back into water.

A Riddle

The tall Wood twins
grip each other everywhere:
"It's all right, we're only
standing in for Lady Stair."

Sound Bites

Attended by thousands, the Sun is opening

———

it's a body-prayer, a shower: you're
in touch all over, renewing, enfolded in a wing—

———

My sorrow, only ninety-five thousand
welcomes left in Scots Gaeldom now.

———

Poor cultures can afford poetry, wealthy cultures can't.

———

Sex is the ever-appeased class
system that defeats Utopias . . .

———

but I bask in the pink that you're in (Repeat)

———

one day, as two continents are dividing
the whole length of a river turns salt.

———

What's sketched at light speed
thunder must track, bumbling, for miles

———

If love shows you its terrible face
before its beautiful face, you'll be punished.

———

People watching with their mouths
an increasing sky-birth of meteors

———

Y chromosomes of history, apologise to your Xes!

Young General MacArthur in a Coonskin Coat

Douglas MacArthur in a raccoon coat,
the Boy Brigadier with slackened cap-seam,
the Fighting Dude, his thin trench whip
and ten-foot scarf strike an English note:
he's the folksiest prince on this troopship.

Nothing here is irony. No returning to the grind
and camping up the glory one last drag time.
His eyes on the camera, his lips twinkle for them.
He'll always be a portrait disguised as a figure;
here he sails to the Jazz Age as the doughboys snigger.

He'll drive them from D.C. when their need scares him,
"It's the orders you disobey that make your reputation!"
yet be sparing with their sons in his bigger war.
As a remake of the Sun God he'll remake Japan,
demand another victory and get made an old man.

You can't see MacArthur past his MacArthur life.
We look from the future. It makes him monochrome
but he's just seen the Elephant, without reversal,
and it's confirmed his genius: total rehearsal.
With himself on each arm he is Hero and Wife.

In the Costume of Andalusia

Traditional costume puts you
anywhere in its span:
was it in the eighteenth
or the twentieth century
you were photographed, in colour,
at noonday in Seville?

Strolling with your sister
or your schoolfellow, perhaps,
and wearing for your *paseo*
the sash of a horsewoman,
the cropped black coatee
and the levelled flat hat.

That day was your perfection,
your tan face unwrinkled
as the rain-coloured skin
of the tiny pearls that buttoned
your ears and white collar.

You were photographed by a man,
a personable foreigner.
The total attention
in your olive eyes,
the stilled line of your mouth
all equally reveal it.

The windows of your perfectly
vertical nose inhale man
but you evince none
of the arts of cliché.
Your gaze photographs
the effect of his gaze and yours.

If you had a name, we might
imagine you strolling on
into all your private pictures,
the Sierra, the Range Rover,
into time's minute razors.

Here, where you still are
as you were then, briefly being
the temper of a people,
you don't know when you're kissed

or when your burnished horse
was brought, block by block,
shuddering happily in the sun.

Chanson

The sun tunes out stars
when it shines the air blue
but the stars burn all day
and you're in their view

the star in your window
among the bow sashes
would itself be a beau
with glitter and dashes

he'd swim in through panes
framed up like the turrets
of old bombing planes
he'd intrude on your merits

as light on a diamond
of VVS grade
diamond's tender to light
brick and wool they are hard—

he's a daylight star though
from far back in time and
those vanish in sun-bleach
so he's all blast and reach

in illimitable night
he'd rather be a highlight
the stars burn beyond day
and you're in their view

The Long Wet Season

Poetry is apt to rise in you
just when you're on the brink
of doing something important,

trivially important, like flying
across the world tomorrow—
while here our paddock, waterlogged

from features and supplements of rain,
smells to be making dark beer
out of rock oils afloat round its grass.

Paperbark trees sleep their lives here.
One supports a flowering constrictor
vine fit to muscle over a rainforest:

that tree's been allowed decades
of half life, being all the vine found,
and the ownerless local flock

of geese, spooked by something, all
glide off like Chinese pottery
spoons, rotating gloved feet.

Out of the sky, crackling and folding
like a spread of the *Australian*,
A snowy egret arrives to spike water.

Nature, getting around like word.

Autumn Cello

Driving up to visit April
who lives on the Tableland
we were sorry for russet beef cattle
deciduous on pasture hills.

We'd had to shower off summer
to climb to the Tableland
where April would be breezily
scuffing her yellow shoes.

As we crossed the caramel river
that is walled in nettle trees
and drove up through black rainforest
the moon was in our mind

it being the dark of the moon
all day, as we went up to April,
the fat moon who saw it is children
who bring death into the world

and was exiled to the sky for it
before there was any April
to plant elm trees, or touch
amber glasses with a spoon.

Next night, the moon would rise
asleep in his brilliant rim
of cradle above bared trees
and April, having forgotten

she was once herself a moon,
would feed cognac-coloured rosin
to her cello bow, and read us
story-feeling without the stories

and straight depth with no sides,
all from her tilted quatrain
of strings with its blunt prong
in her Wilton rug on the Tableland.

Four Character Porcelain Ode

Good to be sane
even in remnant years
left over after demons.
Good to end sane

sitting on curvy rock
in autumn-coloured robe
with teapot and cup
one box of book.

Robe covers sloppy joe
rock merges into clouds
usual effect. Dow Jones
isn't the entire Dao.

Born a Monday child
in woe-filled century
after wars affluent woe
prefers sex weapons. Indulged

rejection is the assault
whatever is victims' fault
comes after, not before.
Fashion paints ashen, scholars.

Absorbed by icicle porcelain
by-appointment Jesuit ware
of the Kangxi reign
unsmashed by Palace experts

Red-Haired South Sea
Demon sage reflects on
bicycle-in-hessian-bag
outline of his nation

dingo in silk trouser
spirit of its gentrification
then watches skinny trees
get exercised by wind

writing knots and switches
across weather of all
four planetary glaze-colours
alumina water silica life.

Sanity's clear sight
of self only temporarily
in the national vitrine
containing no-one older

perturbs less. Celebrity times
resemble Red Guard times
museums purged of past
dead poets not reprinted

James McAuley, David Campbell,
Shaw Neilson, Francis Webb,
Lesbia Harford, Roland Robinson,
achievers free from unison

all out of print
smash! the old china
each who dies now
dies as a commodity

signs no more petitions.
Sip tea, sleep bone
consciousness returning looks like
first particles, then text.

Zengxi said Dao
is friends talking happily
returning from a festival.
No more can do.

The New Hieroglyphics

In the World language, sometimes called
Airport Road, a thinks balloon with a gondola
under it is a symbol for *speculation*.

Thumbs down to ear and tongue:
World can be written and read, even painted
but not spoken. People use their own words.

Latin letters are in it for names, for e.g.
OK and H_2SO_4, for musical notes,
but mostly it's diagrams: skirt-figure, trousered figure

have escaped their toilet doors. *I* (that is, *saya*,
ego, watashi wa) am two eyes without pupils;
those aren't seen when you look out through them.

You has both pupils, *we* has one, and one blank.
Good is thumbs up, thumb and finger zipping lips
is *confidential. Evil* is three-cornered snake eyes.

The effort is always to make the symbols obvious:
the bolt of *electricity*, winged stethoscope of course
for *flying doctor*. Pram under fire? *Soviet film industry*.

Pictographs also shouldn't be too culture-bound:
a heart circled and crossed out surely isn't.
For *red*, betel spit lost out to ace of diamonds.

Black is the ace of spades. The king of spades
reads *Union boss*, the two is *feeble effort*.
If is the shorthand Libra sign, the scales.

Spare literal pictures render most nouns and verbs
and computers can draw them faster than Pharaoh's scribes.
A bordello prospectus is as explicit as the action,

but everywhere there's sunflower talk, i.e.
metaphor, as we've seen. A figure riding a skyhook
bearing food in one hand is the pictograph for *grace*,

two animals in a book read *Nature*, two books
inside an animal, *instinct*. Rice in bowl with chopsticks
denotes *food*. Figure 1 lying prone equals *other*.

Most emotions are mini-faces, and the speech
balloon is ubiquitous. A bull inside one is dialect
for placards inside one. Sun and moon together

inside one is *poetry*. Sun and moon over palette,
over shoes etc. are all art forms—but above
a cracked heart and champagne glass? Riddle that

and you're starting to think in World, whose grammar
is Chinese-terse and fluid. Who needs the square-
equals-diamond book, the *dictionary*, to know figures

led by strings to their genitals mean *fashion*?
just as a skirt beneath a circle means *demure*
or a similar circle shouldering two arrows is *macho*.

All peoples are at times cat in water with this language
but it does promote international bird on shoulder.
This foretaste now lays its knife and fork parallel.

On the Borders

We're driving across tableland
somewhere in the world;
it is almost bare of trees.

Upland near void of features
always moves me, but not to thought;
it lets me rest from thinking.

I feel no need to interpret it
as if it were art. Too much
of poetry is criticism now.

That hawk, clinging to
the eaves of the wind, beating
its third wing, its tail

isn't mine to sell. And here is
more like the space that needs
to exist around an image.

This cloud-roof country reminds me
of the character of people
who first encountered roses in soap.

The Annals of Sheer

Like a crack across a windscreen
this Alpine sheep track winds
around buttress cliffs of sheer
no guardrail anywhere
like cobweb round a coat
it threads a bare rock world
too steep for soil to cling,
stark as poor people's need.

High plateau pasture must be great
and coming this way to it
or from it must save days
for men to have inched across
traverses, sometime since the ice age,
and then with knock and hammer
pitching reminders over side
wedged a pavement two sheep wide.

In the international sign-code
this would be my pictograph for
cold horror, but generations
have led their flocks down and up
this flow-pipe where any spurt
or check in deliberate walking
could bring overspill and barrelling
far down, to puffs of smash, to ruin

which these men have had
the calm skills, on re-frozen
mist footing, to prevent
since before hammers hit iron.

Ernest Hemingway and the Latest Quake

In fact the Earth never stops moving.

Northbound in our millimetric shoving
we heap rainy Papua ahead of us
with tremor and fumarole and shear
but: no life without this under-ruckus.

The armoured shell of Venus doesn't move.
She is trapped in her static of Hell.
The heat of her inner weight feeds enormous
volcanoes in that gold atmosphere

which her steam oceans boil above.
Venus has never known love:
that was a European error.
Heat that would prevent us gets expressed

as continent-tiles being stressed and rifted.
These make Earth the planet for lovers.
If coral edging under icy covers
or, too evolutionary slow

for human histories to observe it, a low
coastline faulting up to be a tree-line
blur landscape in rare jolts of travel
that squash collapsing masonry with blood

then frantic thousands pay for all of us.

At the Falls

High mountain plateau edged
with vertical basalt cliffs
like black hung chain, like sprockets
conveying a continual footage
of water, abruptly curved
and whitening down into clouds.

On a damp earth track
to other viewing points, a
young wife twists her ankle.
She falls painfully. Her husband,
his eyes everywhere like a soldier,
mutters *Get up!* in a panic voice,
Quick! There are people coming.

She struggles up, furious,
spurning his hand. A cloud
like steam rises out of the gorge.
Over years, this memory
will distill its essence: fear

of the house her eccentric man
inhabits, and what is done
there, or away from there.
That she is the human he has married.

The Engineer Formerly Known as Strangelove

Mein Führer, they called me Doctor Strangelove
in the 1960s. This now they'd dare not do.
Right and Left then thought in Perverts, like you
but now it's Doctor Preference, Doctor Paralimbic—

I've also quit the White race. The ac-
cident of pallor became not worth the flak.
I won't join another. Race is decadent.
I lay this wreath on your unknown grave, mein Führer.

In my third sunrise century, Germany
has re-conquered Europe on her knees.
Fighter planes still pull gravities, not levities
but the flag of the West is now a gourmet tablecloth.

The Cold War is a Dämmerung long since of dead Götter
but I am still in cutting-edge high tech.
In a think-tank up to my neck
I rotate, projecting scenarios.

In one, nearly every birth's a clone
of Elvis, of Guevara, of Marilyn
and many later figures. Few new people get born
then nostalgia for nostalgia collapses.

Of your own copies, one is a Trappist, to atone;
the other went through school and never heard of you.
He helps creased, off-register people who fade as they relax.
They are tourists travelling on the cheap, by 3D fax.

Marxists will resurge by squaring sex with equality.
Every wallflower will be subject to compulsory
fulfillment by the beautiful: deprivation makes Tory.
Evolution likewise, that condones and requires

extinctions, will trip the moral wires
of Green thought and become a fascist outlaw.
Darwin will be re-read in tooth and claw.
In another projection, most of life goes Virtual.

War is in space, in the trenches, in chain armour:
for peace, just doff the Tarnhelm. But some maniac
will purloin a real nuke for his psychodrama—
and not the slow old-tech sort you developed, mein Führer.

In that model, too, the screen replaces school,
and language (alas, English) regains the flavourful
and becomes again inventive, once post-intellectual.
Media story-selection and, in the end, all commentary

will be outlawed as censorship. Like fashion
they will be aspects of the crime Assault.
Direct filming of our underlit dreams will replace them
and poverty, sedulously never called a fault,

will be stamped out by the United World Mafia.
Generals and tycoons will be excised like tumors
if they try to impede the conversion to consumers
of all their billionfold peons and garbage-sorters.

To forestall migration, all places will be Where the Action Is.
People will wear their showers, or dress in light and shade.
Australians will learn moral courage, disease will be cured—
Here the Doctor wallowed, and his speech became obscured.

The Images Alone

Scarlet as the cloth draped over a sword,
white as steaming rice, blue as leschenaultia,
old curried towns, the frog in its green human skin;
a ploughman walking his furrow as if in irons, but
as at a whoop of young men running loose
in brick passages, there occurred the thought
like instant stitches all through crumpled silk:

as if he'd had to leap to catch the bullet.

A stench like hands out of the ground.
The willows had like beads in their hair, and
Peenemünde, grunted the dentist's drill, Peenemünde!
Fowls went on typing on every corn key, green
kept crowding the pinks of peach trees into the sky
but used speech balloons were tacky in the river
and waterbirds had liftoff as at a repeal of gravity.